GW00733773

BE YOUR BEST

KICK START

YOUR WAY TO A HEALTHIER LIFESTYLE

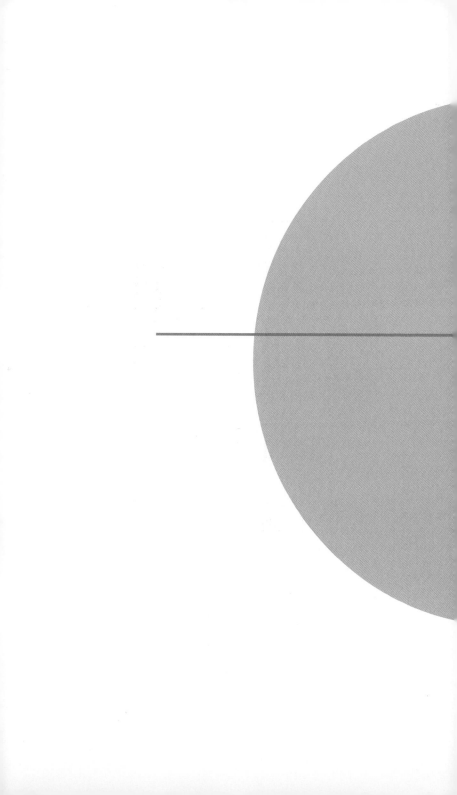

BE YOUR BEST

KICK START

YOUR WAY TO A HEALTHIER LIFESTYLE

Sally Gunnell

with Tim Newenham
and Catherine Larner

Published by:
Crown Sports PLC
33 Imperial Way
Purley Way
Croydon
Surrey
CR0 4RR
Internet: www.crownsportsplc.com
Email: sally.gunnell@crownsportsplc.com

Copyright © 2002 Sally Gunnell

All rights reserved. This publication is copyright and may not be resold or
reproduced in any manner (except excerpts thereof for bona fide study
purposes in accordance with the Copyright Act) without the prior consent of
the Publisher.

Every effort has been made to ensure that this book is free from error or
omissions. However, the Publisher, the Authors, the Editor, or their
respective employees or agents, shall not accept responsibility for injury,
loss or damage occasioned to any person acting or refraining from action as
a result of material in this book whether or not such injury, loss or damage
is in any way due to any negligent act or omission, breach of duty or
default on the part of the Publisher, the Authors, the Editor, or their
respective employees or agents.

ISBN 0-9542724-0-4

Cover & Page Design: Bigg Design
Printed by
L&S Printing
Hazelwood Trading Estate
Worthing West Sussex

CONTENTS

6 Introduction

THINKING IT THROUGH
10 Great expectations
12 Overcoming your fears
14 Goal setting
16 Go for your goals
18 Positive thinking
20 What to expect at the start
22 Personal reward points

74 Walking
76 Running
78 Cycling
80 Cross training

GETTING STARTED
24 Your health check
26 Warm up
28 Stretching
36 Measuring your fitness
38 Home exercises
52 Confidence building

EATING WELL
82 A healthy diet

REST AND RELAXATION
88 Helping your body recover
90 Sit back and relax
92 Massage

IN THE GYM
54 Strength
56 Using the equipment
72 Aerobic

94 Crown Sports Club list
95 Index and acknowledgments

Disclaimer

The author may give opinions and make general or particular statements in this book regarding potential changes of lifestyle habits. You are strongly advised not to make any changes or take any action as a result of reading this book without specific advice to you from your Doctor or Physician.

The Publisher, the Authors, the Editor and their respective employees do not accept any responsibility for the actions of any person - actions which are related in any way to information contained in this book.

INTRODUCTION

Exercise is not about punishing yourself - I want to get that straight from the start! You're not going to be humiliated, embarrassed or worn out. And it isn't a question of learning about all the things you can't do, but finding out about the many more things you can do.

Everyone can benefit from exercise, and everyone can enjoy exercise; it's just a question of finding out what best suits you.

That may be a bit rich coming from an Olympic athlete, you say, but I know as much as anyone about the struggles of keeping fit and healthy. I've had my battles with weight, gone on numerous crash diets in my early 20s, and have had a near-daily struggle getting out of bed to go for a run in the morning.

Now that I've stopped training, I am a working mum with two small children and have all the typical pressures on my day - time is short, I'm torn in different directions and it's all too easy to pick at the wrong types of food and push exercise out of my schedule.

My aims have changed - I am exercising now to keep myself healthy and fit rather than having the goal of a gold medal - but I still have to focus to ensure I keep at it. And I concentrate on knowing how good I'll feel when I do make the effort to look after my body.

It's important to realise what exercise can do for you. I find I get so much more done, make more phone calls, have a clearer head in meetings - and probably shout at the kids much less - if I have taken a few minutes out at the start of the day to go for a run.

But then I expect you bought this book with plenty of ideas for what you wanted to gain from exercise! To lose weight? Get fitter? Well, take this further. Why do you want to lose weight? Is it just a case of getting into the latest fashionable clothes, or will it make you feel better about yourself, give you more confidence? And why do you want to get fitter? To keep up with the recommendations for your age, or to enable you to play football with the kids, walk up the stairs without getting out of breath, have more energy?

How we choose to live our lives impacts every aspect of our daily activities and affects both mind and body. As soon as you take control of your life, by thinking positively, eating healthily and taking regular exercise, you will find that you will gain in confidence, posture, wellbeing and productivity.

Being fitter gives you more freedom and more options. Once you start, you'll find you can tick off a new achievement each week. And as you discover what you are capable of, your confidence will grow stronger and you'll get closer to reaching your full potential.

But before you see this remarkable transformation, you have to acknowledge the power that is going to get you there: YOU. It's your responsibility. So no crying off that the weather's bad, your boss kept you working late, your parents have given you their fat genes, or you don't have time to eat properly.

It's very easy to make excuses, and this is where most people fail. You have to decide how you are going to react when you are faced with barriers. Are you going to turn back or find a way to overcome them?

Together, through the book, we'll explore techniques to help you along, but I believe there are two key things to remember: firstly, what your goals are, and secondly to enjoy it along the way.

Knowing where you are heading is a great motivator. You'll find that you'll be able to put in that little bit more effort if you know that in just two more sessions you'll be reaching your desired weight or fitness.

After I had my second child I decided that training for the Great North Run would be my goal in losing weight. I was raising money for charity, so I couldn't let other people down, and I had a date to aim for so there was an urgency in my training. Then, when it seemed far more appealing to read a magazine than to go for a run, I remembered what I was aiming for and I was spurred on.

I have to confess that fitness has always been part of my life and I still really enjoy going for a run. This means it's so much easier to put on my trainers if I know I'm going to have fun.

A lot of people have terrible memories of sport at school (running round the cross country course in all weathers probably put them off for life!). But think of all the other ways you can get exercise. The growing number of health clubs are introducing a wide variety of new activities to their programmes - have you tried tai chi, yoga or Pilates, group cycling or aquarobics? They're all a good means of exercise but they don't involve pounding a treadmill or getting cold traipsing dark, wet streets. I've had great fun trying lots of sports and activities since I've stopped training. Find out what works for you.

I hope you are looking forward to this new adventure. So let's get going and see what's in store for you!   SALLY GUNNELL

GREAT EXPECTATIONS

Extending your physical capabilities is a wonderful confidence boost, while weight loss and improved strength are a bonus

Your body is amazing! Just take a moment to look at these numbers: 650 muscles, 206 bones, 60,000 miles of blood vessels, not to mention the assorted cartilage, ligaments, skin. There are thousands of tiny pieces all creating a mobile home for who we are and what we want to achieve.

As you get to appreciate the intricacies of your body, I hope you'll treat it with the respect it deserves. Because, if you think about it, looking after yourself is a serious investment which pays dividends faster than any life assurance policy.

Experts say exercise can improve your immune system, so you are ill less often. It increases your mental alertness, lifts your mood, reduces tension and stress, keeps you alert and able to concentrate even as you get older, and makes you feel positive about yourself generally. And, even if you take out just 30 minutes a day to exercise, you will still achieve more overall.

Everyday tasks will be less tiring and you'll cope better with more demanding activities. Walking for longer, and at a quicker pace, without getting so out of breath is something you can look forward to! Regular stretching leads to increased flexibility, so reaching up, twisting and bending should become easier, too.

Don't be surprised if you find yourself tightening your belt after exercising for a while. Your energy reserves (stored as fat) will be diminished by cardiovascular exercise so areas like your waist will change shape.

As muscles in your body strengthen they help protect against injury to them and other parts of the body. The back is particularly susceptible to problems and strengthening muscles in your stomach, sides and back can help prevent back pain.

Your blood pressure will be reduced, cholesterol lowered and conditions such as osteoporosis and diabetes can be controlled or prevented. But be warned, you must exercise regularly. These positive effects are lost if you stop exercising!

OVERCOMING YOUR FEARS

So you know that exercise is good for you, but you've always been held back from doing anything about it because you're frightened of taking those first steps into a gym or exercise class. You don't know what to wear or what to do, and you are afraid everyone will look at you when you walk in the room.

Many people are held back from enjoying life by staying in a comfortable rut; they think it's easier to stay where they are with what is familiar, than to try for something better and fail. Others feel under pressure from their friends and family to conform.

But I urge you to break out of the mould and focus your energy on things that are important to you. Think about what you want - confidence, more energy, better shape, new interests - and go for them. I love this saying: it's better to try 100 things and fail half of them, than try one thing and get it perfect.

There isn't any reason to feel worried or embarrassed about starting out. Remember, it's quite all right to be a beginner and not know the correct way of doing things in an exercise programme straightaway. Set yourself realistic and short-term goals and, as you become confident in doing these basic exercises, your confidence will increase along with your fitness.

Select exercise that suits your personality. If you are shy or self-conscious, concentrate on the home exercises, or buy a good fitness video. If you're competitive and like games, then tennis, squash or football might suit you.

You can combine activities to keep things interesting, and you can incorporate your chosen activity into your daily routine. Cycling, walking or running to work combine a familiar route with your lifestyle change of becoming fitter.

And don't forget, you don't have to do this alone - why not rope in some friends or family and then you can compare notes, encourage each other along the way, and laugh off any little hiccups!

DISPELLING MYTHS

If you think exercise means 'no pain no gain', leotards with thong bottoms, huge, bulging muscles, complicated routines, repetitive movements in a gym, and being made to look silly - don't!

Yes, gyms used to be places for people to strut their stuff. Bodybuilders and athletes would wordlessly compete with each other to prove who was the strongest and the fittest. But not any more - well, not if you choose the right gym!

To me, fitness is a way to get more out of life. And health clubs can help you do that, giving you an attractive environment, variety in the equipment to use, expert advice, and lots of people like you to make friends with.

But you don't have to go to a health club to get fit. The exercises you can do at home, or the lifestyle changes I have suggested can be fitted discreetly into your daily routine.

JOIN THE CLUB

•Choose a gym near your work or home so that it is easy and convenient for you to go.

•Think about the type of health club you will feel comfortable in - do you want big or intimate, women only, family, sporty or social?

•Tour the facilities. Are the machines in good condition? Can you get on the equipment without queuing? Is there a separate stretching area? Are the changing rooms clean?

•Speak to the staff - are they friendly? are there plenty of instructors?

•Before joining, visit the gym at times you would like to work out. It might be busy at peak times.

•Check out the cost and look at how often, and at what times you are likely to visit the gym. Choose a type of membership to suit you.

•Try it out. Most gyms offer passes to potential new members.

GOAL SETTING

Taking control of your body, by keeping fit and healthy, proves that you can do something off your own bat. This is a very positive step and you will find you continue to feel good about yourself as you tone your heart, start to feel more supple and get the endorphins pumping.

Of course, changing your body takes some commitment; you have to stay active and think about your eating patterns. But the one thing which will ensure you make it happen is your mind. So, start off by thinking about what you want to achieve with this programme. By setting yourself goals you can measure your improvement, and will know when to congratulate yourself!

People often overestimate what they can do in a year, and underestimate what they can do in three so, when you're setting your goals, be specific and realistic. And measure yourself against your own personal best, not against other people.

Setting short-term goals is crucial to the long-term success of your fitness programme. Think about what you want to achieve in one or two weeks' time. It should be relatively easy and measurable. It might be 'to go on a 20 minute run', 'to do 10 press ups', or simply 'to enjoy a gym session'. If you have a dream goal, like running a marathon, break it down into more immediate goals which you can achieve within a couple of months. But there's no point aiming for this if you don't like running!

So what are the 12 things that make a difference to your life right now? Write each aspect on a spindle then score the importance of it from 1 (not so important) to 10 (very important). I have put some suggestions in there to get you going!

Now consider how much time you spend on the most important things. Are you spending too much time on low priority areas? How can improved health and fitness improve the quality of these areas?

While you're writing your clearly defined goals, imagine yourself achieving them. It's astonishing but if you believe something hard enough, your brain will assume it's true and then you're half way to making it real. So, by repeating positive phrases, or affirmations, in the present tense, you can trick your brain into thinking you're already the person you want to be. This is even more effective if you picture the scene as well. It's called visualisation and is widely used in sport - I've tried it myself and broke the 400m hurdles world record as a result! It works, so follow the programme, take care of yourself and watch how you become the person you see in your mind's eye.

Most people don't plan to fail, they fail to plan

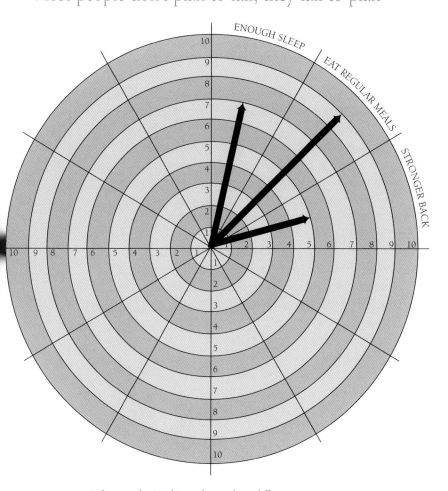

What are the 12 things that make a difference to your
life right now? Write each aspect on a spindle then score the
importance of it from 1 (not so important) to 10 (very important).

GO FOR YOUR GOALS

Well done! You've worked out what you want to achieve. Now we've got to make sure you get there.

First of all, don't underestimate the barriers that keep you sitting on the sofa, or at your computer. Starting a programme of physical exercise is hard enough; maintaining the habit of exercising is even harder. And the biggest obstacle of all is you!

Don't think that I don't know what it's like. That niggling voice that tells you to put your feet up and read a magazine instead of going out for a run? I have it, regularly. Even though I know a quick jog will set me up for the day, it still takes a tremendous effort to finish putting on my trainers.

No matter how many promises you make yourself, and despite being aware of all the obvious reasons for regular activity, that tiny voice can put paid to it all in a flash. But you can control it.

First you must acknowledge that the buck stops with you. It's all too easy to blame someone or something else for your failure. But you have tremendous power in accepting responsibility for yourself. This might seem tough but it's also liberating.

Start now. Tell yourself "this is my life. I am fully responsible for how I live. It's not up to my genes, my family, my income or the weather; it's up to me. I accept this responsibility and I thrive on it."

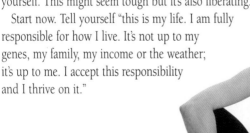

KEEPING GOING

Set processes in place which will help you to stay focused on your goals. These will stop you being easily distracted and ensure you remain motivated by your desire for being your best.

- Find another reason to go to the gym - meet a friend after your workout, for example

- Find yourself a 'workout buddy' who will keep egging you on

Pack your workout kit the night before

- Make an appointment in your diary to exercise

- Keep a record of your activities, your measurements, your thoughts and feelings

- Update your programme regularly

- Book a course of treatments or classes to ensure you get into a regular routine

- If you feel you need individual attention, consider a personal trainer

- Try a new exercise class or activity

POSITIVE THINKING

Now, stop telling yourself what you can't do, and concentrate clearly on what you can and will do.

You have an enormously powerful capability to picture your goals and this, when combined with self-belief, enables your mind to direct you to success. What you see is what you get. Or, as I think Henry Ford once said, "Whether you think you can or think you can't, you're absolutely right".

One of the first tasks is to get rid of the negative voice, your inner critic as psychologists call it. It's meant to protect you by telling you how mediocre you are before anyone else gets the chance and really hurts your feelings. "You'll never win." "You're so fat." Sounds familiar? Whatever you choose to believe, you'll find more evidence for it, and the more you focus on something the more you'll get.

I learned in just a couple of weeks how to control my inner voice. First I had to recognise when it was speaking and then I had to be ready with a response, telling myself how great I was. (It does feel silly at first but then no more so than telling yourself you're stupid). Now I tell myself more positive things each day than negative.

Picture yourself succeeding with an exercise programme - imagine how much more freely you can move, how much stronger you are, and how you can breathe more easily. Imagine a situation with family or friends where you can enjoy life more fully because of this increased fitness. Enjoy the success of achieving your goals, feel comfortable with the idea of success and the congratulations you receive from those around you.

You are going to start on an exercise programme that will make you fitter, healthier and therefore happier. You will succeed. Say to yourself: I am getting more confident with exercise.

Learn how to control your inner voice

As soon as you have a negative thought, write it down. Seeing the things you say to yourself put on paper makes them look ridiculous. Have a good laugh and its power will vanish.

Or put a handful of paper clips in your right pocket first thing in the morning. Every time you think a negative thought, move one paper clip into your left pocket. If you end the day with a pile of paper clips in your left pocket, you'll realise how harmful this is and want to do something about it.

Life deals us certain cards. You can't choose them, but you can choose how to play them, and you can make that choice any time, any place, at any point down the line.

I've always been very determined when faced with an obstacle. Even when something looks impossible, I tell myself 'there has to be a way'.

You can be the same with your attitude to your life - are you going to sit back and blame people and circumstances for your failure, or are you going to fight for what you know you can achieve?

Picture yourself succeeding - what you see is what you get

WHAT TO EXPECT AT THE START

One of the best excuses for failing to start exercising is 'but I haven't got time'. Just take a look at your life at the moment and notice how much time you spend being inactive. You'll be amazed! So it is possible to plan to ensure 30 minutes of moderate physical activity five days a week.

It isn't just a question of making some visits to the gym; it's a lifestyle approach to exercise such as parking your car further away from your office, so you can walk further; using the stairs instead of the lift; getting up 30 minutes earlier, to perform exercises at home. If you are committed to exercising, you'll make the time.

Throughout the book you'll find quick tips to help with your lifestyle approach to exercise, and a personal reward system, to check you are on the right lines.

FEEL GOOD
Wear loose fitting comfortable clothes and ideally give yourself time to shower and freshen up after exercise.

MAKE TIME
Training times can be set to fit in with your lifestyle. Make a date in your diary and keep to it. You are important so don't be distracted by other things. Remember, you are making an investment in your health.

If you can't fit it in one day, try to go for a 10-15 brisk walk just to keep everything ticking over.

Initially you can exercise in and around your home, progressing, if you wish, to joining a health and fitness club that will offer a wider variety of exercises on specialist equipment with expert instruction.

When you start exercising you can expect a number of things to happen: these are normal, healthy responses.

1 Your heart rate increases

As more oxygen is needed by the working muscles, so the heart pumps more blood containing oxygen and nutrients. The harder you work, the more your heart rate increases.

2 You start to feel warm and perspire

Working muscles generate heat. To avoid overheating, water droplets form on the skin which then evaporate drawing heat away from the body. Perspiring is a normal, healthy response to exercise.

3 Your breathing rate increases

As more oxygen is needed by the working muscles, you breathe faster to get more oxygen from the air into the body. Taking deep breaths during exercise is better than short, fast, shallow breaths, so relax and breathe deeply!

4 You feel thirsty

Water from the body is lost through perspiration and every time we breathe out. As you exercise you lose water more quickly, so keep water handy and take sips regularly. You shouldn't feel thirsty at the beginning of exercising, so drink before you start.

HAVE FUN!

Always choose something you enjoy. I couldn't have trained for 15 years if I didn't love it. Maybe you could use your weekends to explore a new activity and let it become a focus for your training sessions in the week.

PERSONAL REWARD POINTS

Starting an exercise programme or lifestyle change usually isn't that bad. In fact, it's quite exciting to do new things and see some early improvements. The hard work starts when the novelty wears off.

The more you stick with it, the better chance you have of maintaining a great routine for life, so gradually adapt successful habits to your own lifestyle - make it work for you.

The key is variety, so experiment with different ways to exercise. Mix up your activities, go for different times, work at different intensities, work out with different people. Develop a store of activities you can call on depending on how you feel or how busy your schedule is. If you don't feel like doing 20 minutes of resistance training, swap in a swim and do the resistance work later in the week. But keep a record of what you have done so you can see you are making progress and are in control of your activities.

It's good to remember that you have responsibility for your actions but, at the same time, you should reward yourself when you have done well, and have made a positive step to a healthier lifestyle. This means you could buy a new item of clothing when you have reached a particular fitness goal, or you could take a weekend break to relax and unwind. Or you could try something that's a little cheaper and more of a daily guide to your progress, like this personal reward tally.

Your aim is to score at least 50 points per week, every week. You'll be amazed at how the points add up just by doing everyday activities, and simply by being conscious of what you do. It's a way of saying well done to yourself for doing the things that will improve your health and fitness and make sure that you keep remembering all the ways in which you can improve your lifestyle.

> The more points you score each week, the better

POINT SCORING

50 points Join a health and fitness club

50 points Change your mattress if it's more than 10 years old

50 points See a chiropodist if you have feet problems

40 points Stop smoking for a month, if you are a smoker

30 points See your GP if you have health concerns

30 points Arrange to see a nutritionist for personal diet advice

20 points Cycle rather than take the car or bus

20 points Take an exercise class

20 points Stretch for 5-10 minutes when you wake up

20 points Swim for 30 minutes

20 points Have a session with a trainer to liven up
your exercise programme

20 points Drink no alcohol for a week

20 points Eat five servings of fruit or vegetables today

20 points Reduce the portion size of your main meal,
if you need to lose weight

15 points Walk your children to school and back

15 points Park your car further away from the office

15 points Use the stairs instead of the lift or escalator for a whole day

15 points Keep a drink of water handy, sip a little and often

15 points Plan your meals in advance

15 points Don't put salt on your food

15 points Plan a quality rest and recovery activity

15 points Have a massage

15 points Use a sauna or steamroom

10 points Have a healthy, high carbohydrate energy snack handy

10 points For each glass of wine, drink a glass of water

10 points Drink a glass of water when you wake up

10 points Sit upright throughout the day, shoulders relaxed and back straight

10 points Rather than carry one heavy bag, balance by using two bags

10 points Play 18 holes of golf

10 points Make your own food instead of using a ready-made meal

10 points Buy food with no added salt or sugar

5 points Practise breathing deeply and rhythmically for five minutes

5 points Play with your children for 30 minutes, without interruption

5 points Phone a friend and go for a walk together

5 points Set your alarm 10 minutes earlier and have breakfast

YOUR HEALTH CHECK

It's never too late to become more active. Men who take up exercise in their retirement, for example, are said to cut their risk of dying from heart disease over the next four years by a third.

But if you have not exercised before, or you are a man over 40 or a woman over 50 and plan to do strenuous exercise, check first with your doctor and have a proper fitness assessment.

If you have any health problems, such as the ones listed below, it is safest to check with your GP before you start. In addition, you should not exercise if you are undergoing any medical treatment, are taking drugs or are in pain from an injury, or if you have just eaten a large meal, or are feeling unwell.

Start gently and build up slowly, particularly if you haven't been active for some time. Remember that any activity is better than none. And little changes can make big differences.

**CHECK WITH YOUR
GP IF YOU SUFFER FROM**

Chest pains, high blood pressure
or heart disease

Chest trouble, like asthma or bronchitis

Serious back problems, such as a slipped disc

Painful joints or arthritis

Diabetes

Recently had an illness or operation

Doubts about your ability to exercise

WHAT ABOUT MY BACK?

You may be reluctant to start exercising because you are
worried about damaging your back. About 60 per cent of us
suffer from back pain at some time during our lives.
It is natural to be concerned about looking after your back,
but being over-cautious might actually cause you more harm.
Injuries often occur because the muscles surrounding the
spine are too weak to support it. If you strengthen the trunk
area, your muscles will do the work instead of your spine,
saving it from overload.

DOESN'T IT HAVE TO HURT TO DO ANY GOOD?

To make physical improvements, you have to push yourself
continually. Your muscles only get stronger and your lungs get
bigger if you give them a slightly harder challenge every week. You
should learn to listen to your body - it is good to feel that you are
putting in some effort, but if something feels wrong, or as if it's not
working properly, then stop and seek professional help.

HOW LONG WILL I HAVE TO WORK OUT FOR?

I don't expect you to become a slave to exercise, working out twice
a day, six days a week. Rather, the idea is to integrate the exercise
into your normal life and to enjoy it. Experts agree that 30 minutes
of moderate activity at least five days a week significantly improves
health and wellbeing. It can also hold down or prevent weight
gain. Combining moderate activity with a sensible, low fat, eating
plan certainly helps weight loss.

WARM UP AND COOL DOWN

Before you rush out the door for a sprint round the block or a
five mile bike ride, stop! The key to a successful exercise
programme is the preparation you do beforehand.

By gently warming up before you start stretching and
exercising, you will get more benefit from training and will be
less likely to feel stiff or tired while you are doing it, or
afterwards. When muscles are warm you can stretch them more
easily and you're able to move more freely.

You should also remember that if you stop exercising
suddenly, your muscles can seize up,
becoming tight and uncomfortable.
A cool down will help reduce muscle
stiffness and reduce the tendency to
feel dizzy, so treat it as part of your
session, don't miss it out!

1

Spend at least five minutes getting the blood flowing through your muscles, making them pliable. You can do this in any number of ways. Merely swinging your arms will do the trick, or you could do some walking or cycling, go up and down stairs a few times, or even vacuum the carpet - that's sure to get the blood pumping! Whatever you choose, aim for a comfortable level.

2

This is also a good time to prepare mentally for your workout - to calm down and focus on what you're about to achieve.

3

At the end of your exercise session, you should take the same approach to cool your body down. So for the last five minutes of an aerobic session, gradually wind down, or make the most of your warm muscles by doing some stretches.

STRETCHING

Flexibility is the most neglected part of fitness but, believe me, it's important. Whatever activity you want to take on, whether it's gentle jogging or Olympic hurdling, your muscles must be prepared for any position you demand of them. Stretching imitates the moves in a smooth and controlled manner.

You already know how to stretch - even if you were living a completely sedentary life, you'd stretch every day automatically when you got up from your desk, after a long journey, even from your bed. In order to ease your stiffness, you move things slowly, gently, pulling your body taut. You stretch what feels good, for as long as it feels good to do so.

By carrying out some simple actions, then, you can help prevent injury and ensure maximum performance. And you don't have to take my word for it, scientists have found that stretching your joints is vital in supporting the strength and cardiovascular exercise you do. You will improve your posture, relieve aching and tight muscles, and prevent many joint problems, particularly back pain. Muscle stretches can teach you how to walk taller and literally look thinner.

If you need more convincing, consider this: injury and inactivity cause stiffness and we can expect to lose 40 per cent of our range of movement between the ages of 20 and 70. However, we can all improve our flexibility, no matter how stiff we are.

An ideal stretching programme would take all the parts of the body through their full range of motion - but that's asking a bit much, so most people settle for consistent, regular stretching of the muscles and tendons that work the major joints, or those that are used the hardest.

It is important to stretch when the muscles are warm. This is when they are most flexible and relaxed, and when the blood is moving. Don't stretch to warm the muscles up; it won't work. So, first cycle for a few minutes if you're in the gym or, if you're at home, take a warm bath.

Make sure you are wearing comfortable clothing and breathe deeply when stretching.

You should try to complete this series of stretches on a daily basis if possible, and always before exercising - it only takes about five minutes.

SIDE STRETCH/A

Stretching your joints is vital in supporting the exercise you do

SIDES AND GROIN
•Stand with your feet wide apart and your arms out by your sides.
•Bend towards your right leg so your left arm points straight up.
•Hold for five breaths, then change sides.

SIDE STRETCH/B

BACK STRETCH/A

BODY TALK
Always listen to your body.
Stretch deeply enough so you can
feel it without hurting and work
within your own limits. After
your first stretch, take a breath,
exhale and try to push a tiny bit
further. Hold each stretch for 20-
30 seconds in total. Just one
stretch is enough for each
muscle group.

BACK STRETCH/B

SHOULDERS, BACK AND GROIN
BACK STRETCH/A
•Kneel on your right knee, with
your left foot in front on the ground
bent at the knee to 90 degrees.

BACK STRETCH/B
•Stretch your arms up above your
head then gently reach back.
•Hold for five breaths then change
knees and repeat.

THIGHS
•Use your left hand to support yourself against a wall, or by holding the back of a chair. Make sure you keep upright.
•Bend your right leg at the knee and hold the ankle with your right hand.
•Keep standing tall, gently stretching your leg.
•Hold for five breaths and repeat with your left leg.

WITHIN REACH
If you cannot reach ‿ur ankle, loop a rolled up ‿el around it and gently raise ‿ foot behind you by holding ‿th ends of the towel and pulling up slowly.

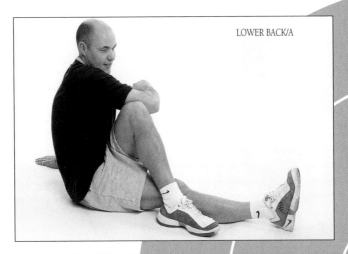

LOWER BACK/A

LOWER BACK/A and B
• Sit with your right leg in front of you and, bending your left knee, place your left foot outside your right thigh.
• Support yourself on your left arm, hand placed on the ground behind your bottom.
• Place your right elbow outside your left thigh and turn to your left, using your right arm to help you.
• Hold for five breaths, change sides and repeat.

LOWER BACK/B

UPPER BACK AND SHOULDERS/A

UPPER BACK AND SHOULDERS/A
•On all fours, with your hands
under your shoulders, drop your
weight onto the right arm.

UPPER BACK AND SHOULDERS/B
•Slide the left arm under the right
arm which then bends.
•Allow the shoulders to drop, relax
the head, and hold for five breaths.
•Repeat, stretching the right arm.

UPPER BACK AND SHOULDERS/B

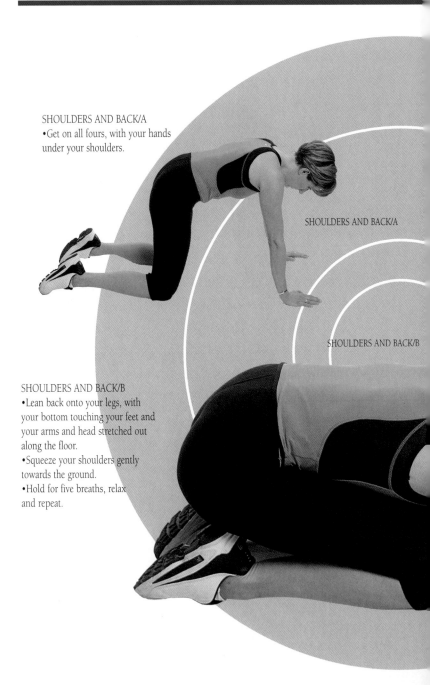

SHOULDERS AND BACK/A
•Get on all fours, with your hands under your shoulders.

SHOULDERS AND BACK/A

SHOULDERS AND BACK/B

SHOULDERS AND BACK/B
•Lean back onto your legs, with your bottom touching your feet and your arms and head stretched out along the floor.
•Squeeze your shoulders gently towards the ground.
•Hold for five breaths, relax and repeat.

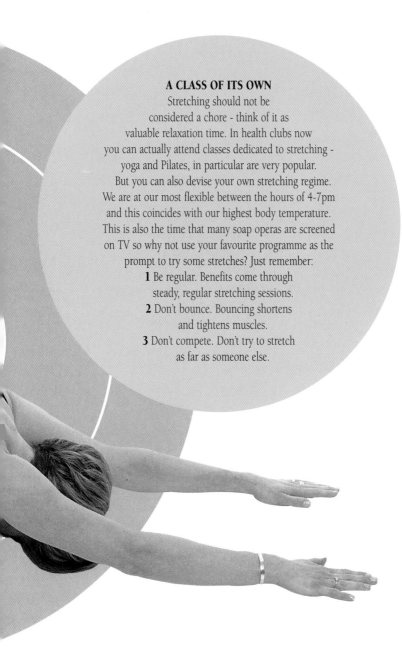

A CLASS OF ITS OWN

Stretching should not be
considered a chore - think of it as
valuable relaxation time. In health clubs now
you can actually attend classes dedicated to stretching -
yoga and Pilates, in particular are very popular.
But you can also devise your own stretching regime.
We are at our most flexible between the hours of 4-7pm
and this coincides with our highest body temperature.
This is also the time that many soap operas are screened
on TV so why not use your favourite programme as the
prompt to try some stretches? Just remember:

1 Be regular. Benefits come through
steady, regular stretching sessions.

2 Don't bounce. Bouncing shortens
and tightens muscles.

3 Don't compete. Don't try to stretch
as far as someone else.

MEASURING YOUR FITNESS IMPROVEMENTS

How you feel about exercising is a good indicator of how you are progressing; an exercise that you thought of originally as being 'somewhat hard' could change to feeling 'fairly light' over time - indicating you are succeeding with your fitness improvements.

Here's a quick way of checking your progress. Choose a walking route that is familiar to you, one that takes 20-30 minutes to cover. Before you start your exercise programme, time yourself walking this route briskly, and score yourself on the scale listed on the next page, known as the Rating of Perceived Exertion (RPE). Write it down.

Walk the route again after four weeks of exercising. Time yourself and score yourself on the RPE scale again. How did you feel: were you quicker or did you feel you used less effort? Were you able to move more easily?

You may like to score yourself for other everyday activities - 30 minutes of mowing the lawn or gardening perhaps. Score before and after starting your exercises. Do you feel more energised? Are you less stiff generally?

KEEP A RECORD

Find a way of keeping a training log. It can work as a planner and a diary, all in one. Fill in your intentions for two or four weeks at a time and note down after each session what you achieved and how you felt. It's important to keep track of what you have done, or what you are having difficulty with. Day by day changes happen almost imperceptibly so if you don't write things down you are unlikely to notice and may get disillusioned. But if you are able to look back on your progress after a couple of weeks you'll get a real buzz from seeing how you have improved.

LEARNING YOUR SCALE

Exercise scientists have come up with a scale where you can measure the amount of effort you are putting into an activity. It is called the Borg Scale or the Rating of Perceived Exertion (RPE).

It is quite straightforward to follow. The only thing worth mentioning is that it starts at 6 and finishes at 20! This is because it corresponds to approximate heart rates - 6 refers to 60 heart beats per minute.

You don't have to measure your heart rate to follow this scale, you just have to keep track on how your body is reacting to the challenges you are setting it.

In the exercises I have given you, I tell you how hard you should work according to this scale

RPE SCALE

6
7 very, very light
8
9 very light
10
11 fairly light
12
13 somewhat hard
14
15 hard
16
17 very hard
18
19 very, very hard
20

HOME EXERCISES

Don't be nervous about starting to exercise - your body thrives on movement, that's what it's designed to do! But if you're worried about having to join a gym to do it - don't be. There are a number of exercises that you can do in your own home - just bear in mind you won't have an instructor on hand to give you expert advice or other people exercising with you helping you on your way. It does sometimes make it easier to have the motivation and support that a gym often provides.

But for now, clear a space so that you won't be bumping into the sofa or television, and where you're unlikely to be disturbed. Make sure that you have a mat or rug to lie on, that the temperature of the room is not too hot or too cold, and that you are wearing comfortable clothing.

Don't be distracted by other things - it's funny how washing the car or doing the ironing can suddenly become incredibly appealing! Be firm with yourself; plan in your exercise time and give it the value it deserves.

Keep track of when you exercised and what you achieved as this will help you spot any patterns. You'll see what you enjoy, what you have difficulty with, and how you are improving.

Once you have got confident with these moves and have started feeling the difference from exercising regularly, you may then decide you would like to have other people to keep you company. That might be the time to consider joining a gym.

These exercises are designed to be done at home without any equipment and are simple but effective.Build up gradually and always work within your limits

ABDOMINAL STRENGTH
•Lie on your back, knees slightly bent, arms by your side on the floor.
•Keeping the pressure on your back evenly distributed, slowly lift your left foot about 5cm off the ground
•Hold for one breath and lower.
•Repeat with your right foot, and alternate for a total of 20 breaths.

PRESS UP/A

• Lie face down.
• Bend your knees, lifting your feet off the floor.
• Cross your feet at the ankles.
• Keeping your hands in line with your shoulders, place them about 30cm out to each side.
• Keep your back flat, tummy in and chin down. Breathe in.
• As you breathe out, push upwards with your arms so that they are straight.

PRESS UP/A

PRESS UP/B

• Lower your body back down towards the floor.
• Keep your back flat, tummy in and chin down.
• Repeat 10 times and build up to three sets of 10.

PRESS UP/B

FULL PRESS UP/A

FULL PRESS UP/A
Progress to a more difficult, full press up when you feel you are ready.
•Lie with your feet level with your hips, your toes on the floor and hands beneath your shoulders.
•With your back flat, tummy in and chin down, breathe in.

FULL PRESS UP/B

FULL PRESS UP/B
•As you breathe out, push upwards with your arms, then lower your body back down towards the floor so that your arms are bent at 90 degrees.
•Repeat 10 times and build up to three sets of 10.

Elbows and knees work like hinges - they only open so far. Keep your elbows and knees 'soft' or very slightly bent during any resistance exercise, so when you straighten your legs or arms, the joints can't 'lock'.

41

BACK STRENGTHENING/A

BACK STRENGTHENING/A
•On all fours, with your knees below your hips, hands below your shoulders, look at the floor underneath you.
•Curl your opposite elbow and knee, drawing them towards each other and rounding your back.
•Hold for two breaths.

BACK STRENGTHENING/B

BACK STRENGTHENING/B
•Now extend your elbow and knee, reaching with your hand in front of you and your leg behind you. You should aim to raise your arm and leg so they are parallel with the ground.
•Hold for two breaths.
•Repeat with your other arm and leg and continue to alternate for 20 breaths.

If you build a good base of muscle, your body will look better regardless of body fat. It's this tone and definition which gives you shape and makes you feel in charge. Plus, improved strength makes daily life that bit easier. Whatever needs to be lifted or moved - children, groceries, filing cabinets - you'll be able to do it more easily and safely.

BACK STRENGTHENING/A
•Lie face down on the floor, with your
arms by your side and your legs straight.
•Hollow your tummy, breathe normally
and raise your shoulders upwards and
backwards.
•Hold for two breaths, relax for two breaths.
•Repeat for 20 breaths.

BACK STRENGTHENING/A

It's important that this exercise is carried out
gently. To someone watching you, they will
be barely able to see the difference, but you
will be able to feel the muscles working as
your shoulders are raised.

You can look after
your back by taking extra
care when carrying things.
Always bend your knees when you
lift a heavy object. Think about your
posture and keep your back
straight when standing
and sitting.

THIGH STRENGTHENING/A
•Stand with your back against the
wall with your feet about 20cm in
front of you, shoulder width apart.

THIGH STRENGTHENING/A

THIGH STRENGTHENING/B
•Slide down the wall slowly, until
your knees are bent at 90 degrees,
and your thighs are roughly parallel
with the floor.
•Feel your thighs working to no more
than level 13-14 (somewhat hard).
•Hold for two breaths, then slide up
the wall, keeping your back flat.
•Rest for two breaths, then
repeat for 20 breaths.

THIGH STRENGTHENING/B

BREATHE IN

It's a typical reaction when you start exercising to stop breathing correctly. It may be because you're concentrating hard or because the activity is a little unfamiliar to you, but it's worth addressing as breathing incorrectly can actually build up blood pressure and cause fainting.

You won't find it difficult to get into the right pattern of breathing, it just takes a little thought. So breathe rhythmically and deeply, focus on relaxing the shoulder, neck and chest muscles. This will help you to take more air in and force a greater amount of air out in each breath. Once you've achieved it you'll find that by relaxing into the activity and breathing deeply you will perform the movement more easily and effectively.

ARM AND SHOULDER
STRENGTH/A

ARM AND SHOULDER
STRENGTH/A
•Place both hands behind
you on the seat of a chair
with your feet in front of
you and your knees bent.

ARM AND SHOULDER STRENGTH/B
• With your weight supported on both arms and legs, bend your elbows to 'dip', lowering yourself to no more than 90 degrees, bent over two breaths.
• Breathe out as you straighten your elbows, pushing yourself up.
• Repeat six times.

A FIRM BASE
Before starting this exercise, make sure the chair is stable - you could place it next to a wall, for example.

ARM AND SHOULDER
STRENGTH/B

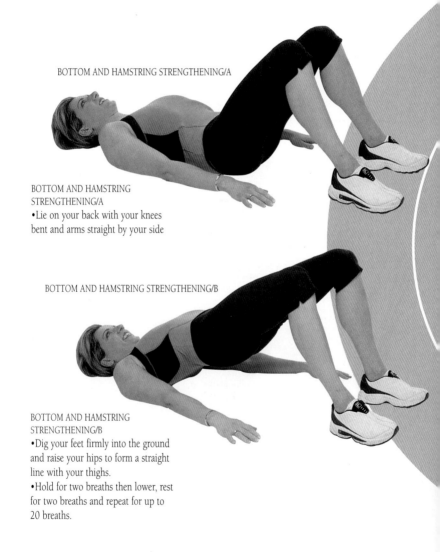

BOTTOM AND HAMSTRING STRENGTHENING/A

BOTTOM AND HAMSTRING
STRENGTHENING/A
•Lie on your back with your knees
bent and arms straight by your side

BOTTOM AND HAMSTRING STRENGTHENING/B

BOTTOM AND HAMSTRING
STRENGTHENING/B
•Dig your feet firmly into the ground
and raise your hips to form a straight
line with your thighs.
•Hold for two breaths then lower, rest
for two breaths and repeat for up to
20 breaths.

ABDOMINAL STRENGTHENING/A
•Lie on your back with your knees bent
and your feet flat on the floor.
•Place your hands on your thighs.

ABDOMINAL STRENGTHENING/A

ABDOMINAL STRENGTHENING/B

ABDOMINAL STRENGTHENING/B
•Slowly and carefully raise your head and
shoulders and reach for your knees.
•Hold for a count of 10.
•Repeat 10 times and build up to three sets.

NECK STRETCH
• Sitting upright in a chair, grip the side of the seat with your right hand.
• Rest the palm of your left hand on the right side of your head, reaching over the top of your head.
• Relax your shoulders and gently pull your head towards your left shoulder, looking forwards all the time.
• Hold for two breaths, repeat on the opposite side, alternating for up to 20 breaths.

BACK STRETCH/A

BACK STRETCH/A
•Stand with your feet comfortably wide apart, knees slightly bent, back straight.
•Hold the towel in front of you, hands twice shoulder width apart, arms straight.

BACK STRETCH/B

BACK STRETCH/B
•Keeping both feet on the ground, rotate slowly to your left to gently stretch the muscles of the back.
•Keep the stretched towel horizontal, hold for two breaths, then repeat, rotating to the right.
•Repeat for 20 breaths.

CONFIDENCE BUILDING

When you take on a new exercise regimen, you deepen your relationship with your body and come to an understanding.

A good workout is a guaranteed way to appreciate what your body can do. When you can run up a hill, you no longer think of your legs as stumpy but powerful, pumping pistons! And after you've taken on a kick boxing class, you're less likely to worry about flabby arms when you can pack a mean punch!

Extending your physical capabilities is a wonderful confidence boost, while weight loss and improved strength follow. You'll find you stand up straighter and naturally command attention.

Confidence in your own abilities shines out of your eyes. If you can laugh and smile with your friends, you'll always be appreciated.

At the same time, I think, it's easier to act with confidence if you know you look your best. Before a race, I used to pamper myself with a shower and hair wash. I'd check my nails and take care over my hair. If you look as though you care about yourself, other people give you respect too.

ACCEPT PRAISE

Now that you're being proactive in improving your lifestyle, you deserve to be admired and congratulated by everyone around you! Tell people how you're getting on; every time you talk about your progress, it's another affirmation for you. Your friends will want to encourage you in your success, so accept praise willingly, with a positive thank you, and remind yourself that you are indeed worthy of this attention.

BE BRAVE!

Don't be afraid of trying new things in front of other people. It can be hard, but even if you're not very good, they'll admire you for having the bravery to give it a go. People will stop looking at the body in front of them and consider your adventurous spirit as your defining characteristic.

GET SUPPORT

With a clear health and fitness goal, and a positive mental attitude, you know where you're going. Surround yourself with people who can support you in your aims. But take care! You may find that someone tries to throw cold water on your enthusiasm. Humans are basically resistant to change and some people may feel threatened by the new, improved you. Tell them about the benefits you'll gain - more energy, less stress, better moods - and suggest they join you.

DON'T PUNISH YOURSELF

If you do slip up by missing out on your sessions in the gym, bingeing on biscuits, or giving up on a particular exercise, don't be too hard on yourself. Treat yourself kindly and spend time doing something you enjoy - take a walk, spend time in the steamroom, or have a soak in the bath. It's not a disaster, just a blip and you'll have plenty of opportunity to make up for it. Don't torture yourself about what you've failed to do, but congratulate yourself for what you have achieved and set yourself another goal.

STRENGTH

Training with weights, or resistance work, can change the way your body functions all day, every day. You'll find that lifting and moving things becomes easier, you lose body fat, your posture improves and you can combat the effects of ageing. And this is the same for men and women.

Every 10 years we lose 5 per cent of muscle tissue and gradually gain body fat. This process can be delayed through exercising regularly. Research has shown that it is possible for deconditioned people to improve their strength by up to 60 per cent after two months of regular training.

Muscle strength can quite easily be increased by using a resistance greater than what you come across in everyday life. The greater the resistance, the more you increase strength - this is called the overload principle.

You can build strength through moving into a stretch position or posture which takes effort to hold still - many yoga exercises are based on this principle. Other exercises that involve movement against resistance also build a very functional strength - sit up exercises using your own bodyweight for resistance is a good example. In the gym, there are a variety of machines which help you to strengthen specific muscles.

Increase in strength comes from an increase in the size of individual muscle fibres, rather than an increase in the actual number of fibres. Training at moderate resistance levels will not have the effect of making you look bulkier, but will help to firm muscles and may change your body shape in a positive way.

It's important to do strengthening exercises regularly, perhaps every other day either at home, in a gym or a mixture of the two. If you stop exercising, the strength gains are gradually lost.

But look at this: one pound of body fat burns just two calories a day, while one pound of muscle burns 35. Muscle just takes more effort to maintain, so the more muscle you have, the more calories you'll burn, whether you're working out or fast asleep.

BENEFITS OF
STRENGTH TRAINING

1 Improved muscle tone
  and physical appearance
2 Improved ability to
  overcome resistance
3 Increased ligament
  and tendon strength
4 Improved body composition,
  more lean body mass
  (body weight minus fat)

USING THE EQUIPMENT

If you decide to join a health and fitness club you will be able to use a range of gym equipment for your strength and aerobic training. In addition, there will be other people with similar interests and aims as you, and you will be able to get individual expert help from qualified instructors who will help you reach your personal goals.

The most important thing to remember is that, before you use any of the machines in the gym, you should ask an instructor for training first. You should also make sure you are using the correct weights for your strength and fitness, and that the machine is correctly adjusted for your height.

There are also a few terms you should be aware of before you begin. When you lift a weight, then lower it back to the start position, that's called a repetition. It's the completion of a single movement. The exercise should have a minimum of eight repetitions and a maximum of 16. But more than 12 indicates you should think about increasing the weight or resistance! A good number to aim for is 10 repetitions for each resistance exercise, and working between levels RPE 13-14 to start with. Perform the exercise over one second and return to the start position over two seconds.

A group of repetitions is called a set. In the past, the most common resistance programme was three sets of 8-12 repetitions. I recommend you only do one set, though, because recent research shows the gains you get from two extra sets is relatively small.

Finally, remember to breathe properly: breathe out as you perform the exercise, breathe in as you return to the start position. Now, off you go!

DRESS FOR SUCCESS
Exercise clothes don't have to be fashionable, but they do need to be comfortable and suited to what you are doing. Baggy is fine, but make sure there is nothing that flaps around and gets in your way. Natural fabrics that breathe are best.

BACK STRENGTH /A

BACK STRENGTH/A
• Curl over the fitness ball, facing forwards on the ground.
• Keep your weight on your arms and ball, and ensure that you are balanced and comfortable.

BACK STRENGTH/B

BACK STRENGTH/B
• As you gently lift your feet off the ground, breathe out.
• Your body should be in a horizontal position - your legs no higher.
• Breathe in as you control your back muscles, returning to your start position.

CHEST PRESS/A

CHEST PRESS MACHINE/A
(ARMS, CHEST, SHOULDERS)
•Sit well back on the seat with both
feet flat on the floor.
•If necessary, adjust the height of the
seat so that your hands are in line with
your shoulders.

If you feel stiffness
in the muscles either the
day after or two days after
strength training, take a couple
of days rest; it's just an
indication that the muscle
is repairing and
rebuilding itself.

CHEST PRESS/B

CHEST PRESS MACHINE/B
•Push the handles forward until your arms are almost straight, taking care not to lock the elbows.
•Breathe out as you push.
•Return to the starting position, keeping your movements slow and controlled throughout, and breathing in.

HIGH PULLS/A (SHOULDERS)

•Hold the low pulley bar with your palms and fingers facing into your body.

•Your arms should be straight and shoulders relaxed.

These muscles are responsible for an upright posture and open shoulders. Good posture not only cuts down everyday aches and pains, but makes you feel more confident too.

HIGH PULLS/A

SEATED ROW/A

SEATED ROW/A (UPPER BACK)

•Sitting with knees slightly bent and arms straight out in front of you, hold the bar with your palms and fingers facing into your legs.

HIGH PULLS/B

HIGH PULLS/B
•Breathe out as you lift the bar to chin height bending your elbows as you lift.
•Breathe in as you move the bar slowly down to the start position.

SEATED ROW/B

SEATED ROW/B
•Keeping your back straight, pull the bar to chest level, while breathing out.
•Control the bar slowly back to the start position while breathing in.

LEG CURL/A

LEG CURL/A
(LOWER LEG)
•Sit well back on the seat and slide your legs in between the two pads. The top one should be resting just below your knee and the lower one should be just above your ankles.
•Hold onto the handles at the side for support.

On average, men have more muscle tissue than women because growth is influenced by the male hormone, testosterone. Weight for weight, men's and women's muscles exert roughly the same force

LEG CURL/B
•Slowly bring your legs
back into your body so
that your knees are at
90 degrees.
•Keeping your movements
slow and controlled, raise
your legs back to the
starting position.

LEG CURL/B

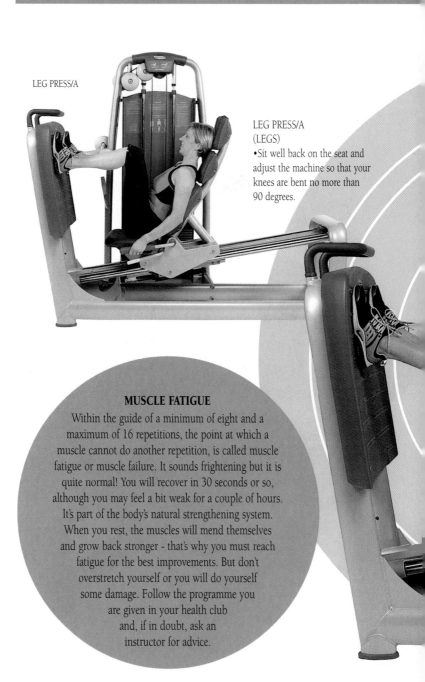

LEG PRESS/A

LEG PRESS/A
(LEGS)
•Sit well back on the seat and adjust the machine so that your knees are bent no more than 90 degrees.

MUSCLE FATIGUE

Within the guide of a minimum of eight and a maximum of 16 repetitions, the point at which a muscle cannot do another repetition, is called muscle fatigue or muscle failure. It sounds frightening but it is quite normal! You will recover in 30 seconds or so, although you may feel a bit weak for a couple of hours. It's part of the body's natural strengthening system. When you rest, the muscles will mend themselves and grow back stronger - that's why you must reach fatigue for the best improvements. But don't overstretch yourself or you will do yourself some damage. Follow the programme you are given in your health club and, if in doubt, ask an instructor for advice.

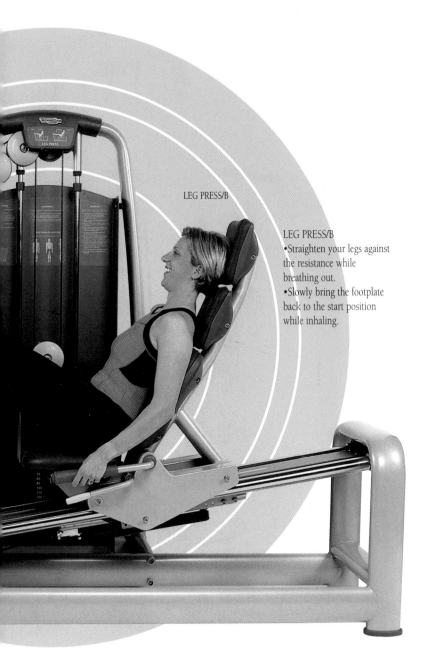

LEG PRESS/B

LEG PRESS/B
•Straighten your legs against
the resistance while
breathing out.
•Slowly bring the footplate
back to the start position
while inhaling.

LAT PULL DOWN /A

LAT PULL DOWN/A
(UNDER THE ARMS)
•Sit facing the machine, with
both feet flat on the floor.
•Hold the bar with your palms
and fingers facing the machine,
at twice your shoulder width.

LAT PULL DOWN/B

LAT PULL DOWN/B
•Keeping your back straight
and your bottom on the seat,
pull down so that the bar is
below nose level.
•Breathe out as you pull.
•Control the bar slowly back
to the start position, breathing
in as you do so.

KEEP FOCUSED
Try not to get distracted by
thoughts of work or other activities
as you work out. Instead, clear your
mind and concentrate on your body;
think about your muscles
contracting, for example.You'll find
you put more effort into your
workout and you'll probably
feel better mentally too.

67

INNER THIGH/A

INNER THIGH/A
(INSIDE UPPER LEG)
•Sit well back in the seat
with your back against
the support.
•Adjust the knee pads
so your legs are
comfortably apart.
•Hold the handles on the
side for support.

INNER THIGH/B

INNER THIGH/B
•Breathe out as you bring
your knees together against
the resistance.
•Keep your bottom and
back firmly against the seat
as you move your legs.
•While breathing in, slowly
move the knees outwards to
the start position.

OUTER THIGH /A

OUTER THIGH/A
(OUTSIDE THE
UPPER LEG)
•Sit well back in the seat
with your back against
the support.
•Your knees should be
together inside the two
knee pads.
•Hold the handles on the
side for support.

OUTER THIGH /B

OUTER THIGH/B
•Breathe out as you press
your knees outwards.
•From the knees apart
position, breathe in and
return to knees together
start position.

69

ABDOMINAL EXERCISES

A well toned tummy - or rippling washboard abs, if you prefer - has always been a highly sought after result from exercising, to a lesser or greater degree. Now researchers say that a strong stomach also benefits the back. This core strength enhances your posture.

There are three sets of muscles running along the front and sides of your torso. You should concentrate on working these muscles in abdominal exercises after your resistance workout. These muscles respond quickly to exercise so you should feel an improvement within two weeks.

Always focus on the effect of your movements. Check it's your abdominal muscles that do the work, never your back, shoulders or neck. Make the movements slow and controlled so momentum can't do the work for you.

ABDOMINAL AND BACK STABILISER/A
(ABDOMEN)
•Slide under the abcurler frame and lie with your back on the mat.
•Bend your knees so your feet are flat on the floor, hip width apart.

ABDOMINAL AND
BACK STABILISER/A

ABDOMINAL AND
BACK STABILISER/B

ABDOMINAL AND BACK STABILISER/B
•Breathe out as you lift your shoulders and upper back off the ground.
•Your lower back should remain in contact with the mat.
•Breathe in as you slowly return to your start position.

OBLIQUES/A
(SIDE MUSCLES)
•Underneath the
abcurler, lie flat on
the floor.
•Bend your knees and
gently swivel the hips so
that your right hip is on
the ground.

OBLIQUES/A

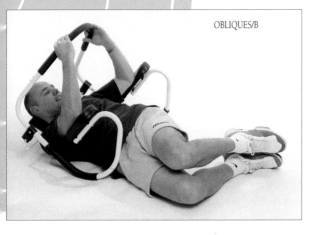

OBLIQUES/B

OBLIQUES/B
•Breathing out, lift
your shoulders and
upper back off
the ground.
•Your lower back
should remain in
contact with the mat.
•Breathe in as you
slowly return to your
start position.

AEROBIC EXERCISE

Aerobic, or cardiovascular, exercise is any activity that works your heart and lungs, making you breathe harder than normal. It includes brisk walking, running, cycling, swimming, housework, tennis, dancing, football, as well as dedicated aerobics classes at the gym.

As you improve aerobically, the muscle fibres surrounding your heart become thicker and stronger, so more blood is pumped with each heart beat. Your blood circulation becomes more efficient, so your heart rate is slower when you are resting.

As with other types of exercising, you need to work at an intensity slightly higher and for longer than you encounter in everyday life to gain benefit. Current recommendations for general health are that everyone should try to take 30 minutes of aerobic exercise five times a week.

Using the RPE scale, you should aim to work at a level of 11-12 for 20-30 minutes - you should still be able to hold a conversation at this level of exertion!

If you really are new to exercise, try training for 2-3 minutes at a time at a 'comfortable' 12 on the RPE scale. Walk slowly or rest for the same amount of time you have exercised. This varied pace training (aerobic interval training) is a great way to start if you haven't exercised for a while and you can raise the level as you gain in fitness. For example, you could jog for two minutes, then run hard for one minute, and repeat several times.

If you are reasonably fit, you should aim to walk/cycle/run for periods of 2-15 minutes at 12-14 on the RPE scale.

You should support your aerobic activity with strength and stretching work to enhance the benefits and help avoid injuries.

Long-term regular aerobic training along with eating the right food (a balanced diet in terms of quality and quantity) helps to maintain a healthy body composition.

BENEFITS OF AEROBIC TRAINING

1 It improves your cardiovascular system: your heart, lungs and the processes they go through to deliver oxygen to your blood, and blood to your muscles

2 Aerobic fitness helps you feel more confident in daily activities such as running for a bus or playing with your kids

3 The longer, slower sessions of aerobic activity help your body to become efficient at using fat for fuel

4 It's fun! Think of the walking, cycling, skating or tennis you can enjoy to improve your aerobic capacity!

WALKING

There are few more effective ways to exercise, and arguably none more pleasant, than simply taking a walk; you don't need any special equipment, and you can do it any time, anywhere!

I don't mean a slow amble, though, or a walk from one shop window to the next! After warming up, you should adopt a vigorous pace, moving correctly and efficiently to get the most benefit. The Americans call this Power Walking.

Walk so that your heel strikes the ground first followed by your foot 'rolling' forwards so you can then push off using your toes, with quite a straight back leg.

By increasing your rate of walking and the length of your stride, you strengthen the muscles of the thigh (called the quadriceps), the back of the upper leg (hamstrings), and the lower leg (calf). Although the pace should be faster than your usual walk, it's important that you are still able to hold a conversation.

Think about your posture as you walk by using the muscles in your stomach and back to keep your body upright. Keep your shoulders relaxed and your chest and head up. Swing your arms as you walk, keeping them bent to about 90 degrees at the elbow, and think of digging the elbows back rather than reaching out in front of you with your hands. This is particularly important for balance if you go up a hill.

Choose a route which has a variety of surfaces - grass, gravel, paths and pavement. This will make your ankles stronger, and can help improve balance. If you include a few hills, your walk will be even more challenging. Don't speed up on the uphill part but get into a good rhythm with deep relaxed breathing. Expect your heart to beat a little faster as you walk uphill or when you speed up your walking pace.

If you choose to join a health club, get the fitness instructors to help you with walking training on the treadmill. Apart from the advantage of walking inside when the weather's bad, treadmills offer a variety of helpful interval programmes.

FEET FIRST

Before you start, check your footwear fits correctly. If your toes are being pinched or the shoes are too big, you risk aching joints and blisters. It's a good idea to wear trainers which will give support and shock absorbency. Get advice from the trained staff at the sports shop or health club to make sure you buy the ones most suited for you. Correctly fitting shoes also help reduce the risk of twisting your ankle. Wear socks with a high cotton or wool content.

RUNNING

If you lift your pace and start jogging or running, you will get an even better cardiovascular workout.

However, running makes a lot of demands on your body; every time your foot lands it sends shock waves through your body of four to eight times your weight. Wearing the right shoes can help reduce this jarring effect on your joints (particularly your knees and back). There are several running styles, so find a pair of shoes which match your particular gait.

When you start running, your heart will quickly start beating faster, but it should then level out if you run at a steady pace. Your body temperature will increase steadily as the working muscles generate heat, and you will start to perspire as your body tries to lose this heat. It makes sense to wear loose comfortable clothing that doesn't resist movement and enables perspiration to evaporate.

It takes around six minutes for your body to adjust to jogging at a steady pace, so do start gently and only increase your pace gradually.

Don't think you have to progress from jogging to running. You will actually burn about as many calories jogging as you would running - it'll just take you twice as long!

Jog or run alternate days so that your body has a chance to recover. You can stretch and do strengthening work on the days when you're not running.

You may decide you'd prefer to jog or run inside on a treadmill. These machines provide a consistent, sprung surface to run on and are usually in a well ventilated position in a gym. They have pre-set programs too, helping make the session more interesting. And they give you feedback on how fast your heart is beating, the speed you are travelling, the distance covered and how many calories you are estimated to use. Jogging at 3.5mph for 20 minutes will burn roughly 100 calories, for example.

BUILD IT UP

If you decide to try running, don't attempt to go flat out for 20 minutes immediately. Build up your pace and duration gradually. Try varied pace training where you walk or jog for two minutes, then run for one minute, and repeat.

CYCLING

If walking or running don't appeal, or if you are overweight, try cycling. Your body is supported and there is no impact, so it is less likely to damage your joints. You can start slowly and gradually build it up and you can incorporate it into your daily schedule - a 20 minute cycle ride to work each day is a good start to fitness and, if you live in a city, you may find it's quicker than the bus or car!

It's fun too of course, but do make sure you get advice from a cycle shop on setting your bike up. A common mistake is having the saddle height too low so the legs never get anywhere near straight. You should have just a slight bend at the knee when you push on the pedal.

Aim to work at around 70 pedal revolutions per minute (rpm), which is just over one turn of the pedal per second. Use your gears to keep at roughly the same pedalling rate. Ideally your bike should have at least 10 speeds to cope with different conditions.

Your cycling action should be rhythmical with a smooth push down on the pedal. Avoid jabbing movements: changing to a higher gear will help. Keep your back straight to take the strain off your lower back, and get the feeling of leaning on your handlebars as you push on the pedals.

Cycling mainly works the quadriceps muscles in the thigh and the calf so make sure you cool down and stretch afterwards to avoid stiffness. Working at around 70rpm helps minimise fatigue too, as it maximises blood flow.

Using an exercise cycle at a health club enables you to work the hamstrings too because these bikes have foot straps on the pedals. As one leg pushes and straightens, the other leg can pull upwards to strengthen the back of the upper leg too.

Many health clubs also offer studio classes where an instructor leads a group of people on stationary cycles in a programme accompanied by music. It is a fun and energetic workout.

INDOOR BIKE

Make sure you are sitting correctly with the seat at the right height for you and positioned so you can pedal comfortably.

Don't set off with the resistance level set too high. Work on your speed first and then increase the resistance.

Exercise cycles have built in programs to simulate going up and down hills, so get advice from the fitness professional to make best use of these features.

CROSS TRAINERS

In the gym, you'll find that the fitness equipment manufacturers have created a variety of machines to help you carry out your aerobic exercise. One of the most recent is the cross trainer.

This is best described as a cross between a treadmill, an exercise bike and a stepping machine. Your feet go up and down, backwards and forwards in an elliptical or oval shaped movement, mimicking the pattern of walking, but avoiding the impact on the joints that happens when you touch the ground.

You can change the movement, so that you are effectively walking backwards on the machine, allowing you to work different muscles - the hamstrings rather than the quadriceps. Some machines also have moving handles so that you can exercise your upper body at the same time.

As you progress through your aerobic exercise, start with cycling where your bodyweight is supported, then try the cross trainer and finally move onto the treadmill.

MIX AND MATCH
You may choose to mix the different types of cardiovascular training - cycling, walking, running and swimming - and start exercising for 30 minutes. Don't be afraid to try new things, but be realistic about what you can achieve. Always choose something you enjoy. I couldn't have achieved what I did, if I didn't love it.
Develop a store of activities you can call on depending on how you feel or how busy your schedule is. Every little helps and you don't have to go flat out - a cycle ride with friends at the weekend will pass a couple of hours easily and enjoyably.

ELLIPTICAL TRAINER
The handles on this machine allow you to partially support your body as you exercise. You are then concentrating on working your leg muscles.

Non-impact exercises, like this one, protect your joints. But you can reduce the risk of osteoporosis when you exercise with impact.

A HEALTHY DIET

The extra exercise you are doing is enough to help you start losing weight. But, as you feel fitter and healthier, you may want to speed up the results by reevaluating your diet as well.

Poor eating can lead to poor fitness, obesity, heart disease and some types of cancer. If that's not enough, eating the 'wrong' foods at the 'wrong' times can lead to very low energy levels, so you end up feeling flat instead of alert and energised.

The whole area of nutrition is huge, but it needn't be complicated - just keep the basic principles in mind when choosing what types of food to eat, and how much to eat.

Understanding what the different nutrients in your food actually do for you will help you to choose more wisely. Start by taking a look at the nutrition labelling on foods.

Eating well isn't hard to do in principle, but it does take thought and planning - if you fail to plan, you'll find yourself snacking on convenience foods for a quick energy fix or depriving yourself of essential nutrients. I know because I've been there.

In my time, I have obsessed about food, been diet crazy and have eaten all the wrong things.

I changed my attitude to food when I moved from the 100m to the 400m hurdles and needed more nutritious fuel for the type of training I was doing. Without even realising it, I cut out the mad diets and started to eat better food consistently.

These days, my eating style is a balance between my past extremes. I enjoy natural, healthy food, plus a few packets of crisps a week! I enjoy going out and the social side of food more than anything. I look forward to my evening meal because I'm going to spend time with family and friends, not because I'll finally be allowed to eat!

So focus on your fitness and let your diet find its own balance. Be aware of the way food affects body shape but don't get wound up about it.

> If you make small, gradual changes you shouldn't ever notice your improved diet, let alone resent it

LOSING WEIGHT

Cutting calories works - it must do. If you eat less calories than you burn off, you'll lose weight.

The thing is, life is too short. And food is too delicious! Converting everything to numbers takes the joy out of eating - if you eat healthy food and exercise regularly you shouldn't have to be this obsessive. However, if you haven't thought much about the food you eat before, it wouldn't hurt to develop an awareness of what's in it.

Labels tell you how much energy is contained in food. It is measured in kilojoules (kj) and kilocalories (kcal) and expressed 'per 100g' and 'per serving' so you can compare. Kilocalories are usually referred to as calories.

The Recommended Daily Average (RDA) intake of energy for men is 2,500kcal and for women 2,000kcal.

Of course, working to an average can be misleading; the exact amount of calories we need depends on our build, age, metabolic rate and lifestyle. The more active you are, the more calories you need to maintain your weight, which is exactly why exercise helps you lose weight.

If you eat more calories than you need then you will tend to put on weight, then remain overweight as the excess energy you eat is stored as fat.

Eating less calories than you need generally results in weight loss as your energy stores are used. Losing too much weight by eating too few calories leads to a wide range of medical conditions as your body cannot function properly.

Your GP can advise you of your personal healthy weight range and it is quite normal for you to fluctuate within the range.

A healthy diet is about moderation and variety. Balance the food you eat with physical activity to maintain or improve your weight

THE ENERGY SOURCE

Carbohydrates in food provide your immediate energy source for everyday life, and there are two main forms: starchy foods, like pasta, rice, potatoes; and sugary foods, like sugar, chocolate, sweets.

The problem with the sugary foods is that they give you a quick energy 'high' then drop your energy levels right down shortly after, to a lower level than you had in the first place.

It's easy to fall into the trap of feeling tired, having a sugary snack, feeling better briefly then feeling low again and in need of another snack. If this sounds familiar, you need to break the cycle!

Starchy foods give you carbohydrate for energy on a slow release basis which keeps you energised for longer without the dramatic energy highs and lows. They also provide dietary fibre that aids digestion. Aim for around 300-400g a day which should represent about 50-65 per cent of calories eaten.

THE RESERVES

Fat - what an emotive word! As a nutrient, fat can be quite misunderstood but it provides a reserve source of energy, regulates temperature and cushions vital organs. Fats also contain vitamins A, D, E and K. So cut out all fat at your peril!

The problem today is that too much fat has been eaten by too many people causing a higher level of obesity and the resultant health problems.

No more than 30 per cent of the calories you eat should be fat, and saturated fat (that is red meat, whole eggs, whole milk and milk products) should represent no more than 10 per cent of calories in your diet. This means that between 30 and 65g can be eaten per day.

THE BODY BUILDER

Proteins are the body's building blocks and they support growth and repair, help in digestion and feed the immune system. They are found mainly in meat, fish, milk products, eggs, soya beans and tofu.

Only about 50-70g of protein is needed daily, representing 12-20 per cent of calories eaten. Younger people need slightly more than adults. Too much, especially animal protein, is bad for kidneys and bones in the long term.

By the way, protein isn't normally used for energy.

DOUBLE CHECK

If you eat healthy food in the right quantities, you shouldn't put on weight. So consider the following.

1 Is your food truly healthy? Some items could be made with more fat than you think.

2 Pure food is safer and more filling than processed food.

3 Vegetarian doesn't always mean healthy. Change cream sauces for tomato, don't overdo the cheese toppings and be wary of sugar and salt content in ready-made meals.

4 Be honest. Keep a food diary for a week and you may find you snack more than you think.

5 Check your quantities - are you eating the family's leftovers?

VITAMINS

There are many vitamins which are needed for our bodies to function properly, and each vitamin has a particular job.

A normal varied diet should give you all the vitamins you need but, if in doubt, consult your GP who may prescribe vitamin supplements.

Vitamin deficiencies are serious. Diseases such as scurvy (lack of vitamin C) and beri beri (vitamin B) are rare today, but there are thousands of other changes that might take place in the body if we lack certain vitamins.

A good diet is a strong defence against bugs. But even once you've got flu or a cold, foods rich in vitamins A, C and E can help.

MINERALS

In small, but essential, amounts, minerals support the formation of bone, nails, teeth and blood cells.

The liver stores most minerals for long periods but if any particular mineral is taken in excess, it can be harmful to the liver, pancreas and heart.

Calcium is well known as being the essential mineral for strong bones, and it also improves heart and muscle function. You don't have to eat a lot of high fat dairy products to get it; go for skimmed milk, low-fat cheese and yoghurt, oily fish canned with their bones, almonds, spinach and sesame seeds.

MAKING IT WORK

1 Ensure all meals have a balance of carbohydrate and protein, and you eat a wide variety of fruit, vegetables, meat, fish and pulses.
Only very sparingly use fats, oils, salt and sugar.

2 If you want to reduce the overall amount you eat, use a two-thirds size plate.

3 Don't feel you have to finish everything on your plate.

4 Plan your meals in advance and plan what snacks you may want to have with you. Make sure water is easily available.

5 If you crave chocolate or sugary food, offer yourself a piece of fruit first. If you don't want it, you're not hungry. If you do, you probably won't want the chocolate any more.

6 Coffee, tea, concentrated juices, and alcohol are all diuretics, that is they help the kidneys eliminate water - so you end up with less water in the body. These are not good for quenching thirst! Water is best.

7 Don't be put off by conflicting views from experts on specific food items, the guidelines I've given you work!

8 Eat five portions of fruit or vegetables each day.

WATER

About 60 per cent of your body is water and, as we can't store it, or make it, but lose water when we breathe, sweat and urinate, we have to keep drinking!

One of the biggest mistakes people make is to wait until they feel thirsty before they drink. By then the body is already dehydrated. Aim to keep water with you all the time so you never get to the point where you feel thirsty.

You can't drink too much water but you should aim for at least two litres, which is about eight glasses. It seems a lot at first, but after a couple of weeks it will become much easier.

I have a glass of water first thing when I wake up, to counteract the dehydration that happens overnight, and then some with every meal - so that's four glasses straightaway!

HELPING YOUR BODY TO RECOVER

So you've stretched and exercised to make yourself stronger, leaner and more agile. Now comes an enjoyable, but often neglected part of training - the recovery sessions.

Actually I've always found this really hard! I'm constantly on the go and have to force myself to sit down even for half an hour. But athletics taught me that taking time to chill out is an important part of reaching your personal best. Rest time allows your body to recuperate and grow stronger, leaving you recharged and hungry for the next session.

As a working mother, I've found this principle still holds true. I know Finley gets a better quality of mum when I'm re-energised, than when I'm tired and overstretched. Although relaxation time might mean time for you, it's not selfish at all.

Like fitness, relaxation is an investment. Would you rather take time out when you choose to, or have it forced upon you by exhaustion or illness?

Avoid working at weekends, staying out too late, and get plenty of sleep. I was always told that eight hours a night was best, but quality is better than quantity so make sure you wake up feeling thoroughly rested.

Aim to spend at least one week a year doing something completely different. Take a holiday - and give yourself chance to enjoy it! Don't go so stressed out that it takes you the whole time to recover, and choose activities to help you unwind.

But, as with exercise, you don't need a huge amount of time to relax. Find moments during your day - five minutes in a morning, half an hour in the evening or a luxurious two hour stretch at the weekend.

You can choose from a range of reviving and revitalising recovery activities from a simple 30 minute walk plus stretching, to a cycle ride or a soak in a hot bath. If you decide to join a health club, you'll find more activities open to you.

SWIMMING

Swimming is good for cooling down after exercising and for a relaxing recovery session. The buoyancy of the water means that the muscles used when we stand can relax for a change.

Try swimming rhythmically at a slow to medium pace, focusing on relaxed breathing to get the most benefit. You may use a float if you wish, or wade through waist to chest high water swinging your arms to help relax the muscles.

Swimming is a great all round activity - it tones your legs and arms and strengthens your tummy muscles and back, as well as being a great aerobic exercise. So you may like to fit it into your programme alongside the cycling, running and walking.

SIT BACK AND RELAX

It is well known that warmth helps muscles to relax and, if you are in a quiet, enclosed and secure environment, it is easy to wind down and let the mind switch off. This is why a long soak in a bath can be so rewarding. Health clubs provide some great alternatives though, with the spa bath, sauna or steamroom.

The heat in the sauna or steamroom will probably be more intense than you are used to in your bathroom, but it will help you relax, ease tired or sore muscles, and also cleanse the skin.

Whichever of the three facilities you choose to try, you should always shower before going in, stay only as long as you feel comfortable and, afterwards, make sure you take a cool shower. It is also important to drink plenty of water.

SAUNAS

It's hot and dry in a sauna so you will quickly start sweating, clearing out your body's toxins and cleaning the pores. It's usual to go out for a cool shower after a few minutes to wash and lower your body's temperature.

The hottest part of the sauna is opposite the coals and on the higher benches. To make it even hotter, you can drizzle small amounts of water over the coals, using the ladle and bucket provided.

Remember though, it's not an endurance test to see how long you can stay in the sauna; you should cool down if you feel uncomfortable.

STEAMROOMS

Unlike the 'desert' heat and low humidity of the sauna, the steamroom has a more 'tropical' atmosphere with very high humidity.
Your body's response to the warmth is to sweat, but because the air has a lot of water vapour, or steam, the sweat cannot evaporate from the skin. This film of what is mainly water covering the body adds to the warming effect, helping to relax the muscle tissue.
The added benefit of the steamroom is that breathing warm, moist air can also be good for your general health. Many health clubs add essence to the steam, and eucalyptus is particularly soothing.

SPA BATHS

Hot tubs with water jets can be one of the most relaxing areas in the health club.
As well as the warmth penetrating deep into tired muscles, the movement of the water from the jets gently massages the muscle tissue.

MASSAGE

The healing power of touch has been known for thousands of years. In fact, it is instinctive: a mother will place her hand on her baby when it is sick; when you fall over as a child, you're told to rub it better; and in cold weather you rub your arms and legs to keep warm.

Massage is now widely available in health clubs and day spas and is considered one of the best ways to relax after you've had a workout, taken part in sport, or even just had a hard day at the office.

By improving your circulation, massage helps you get rid of toxins such as lactic and carbonic acids. These often accumulate in the muscle fibres and cause aches, pains and stiffness.

There are many different sorts of massage ranging from the gentle and relaxing to the vigorous sports massage - which is not for the faint hearted! Regular full-body massage (at least twice a month) is especially beneficial to people who lead less active lives.

You shouldn't underestimate the emotional effects of massage either. Aromatherapy massages are very popular today and are widely available, using the power of smell to trigger emotions and memories. Oils extracted from plants, flowers, trees, and fruit each have special properties. A therapist can mix and match these essential oils to suit your mood, health concerns and preferences. If chosen correctly, these can help you relax, revive and heal your body.

You can also apply the principles of aromatherapy yourself. I first tried it when I heard it could help me relax before a big race. The more I wanted a good night's sleep, the harder it was to unwind. So, the next time, I put a few drops of lavender oil in my bath and a few on my pillow and I fell asleep straightaway!

I try to have a massage every couple of weeks and always leave feeling like a new woman, relaxed yet alert. I also swear by it for preventing illness and always book a massage if I feel a cold coming on. However, it is not wise to massage inflamed skin or joints, varicose veins, swellings, bruises, torn muscles, broken bones or burns.

Find out if your local health club offers a range of treatments, or ask your partner to gently massage your body.

DO NOTHING

If you close your eyes and breathe deeply for a few moments, you'll focus better on what you're doing now, instead of the six million things you have to do next. If you use relaxation time to tap into your mind, it comes back with more ideas and solutions for your problems. You might like to try relaxation classes if you really find this difficult. These will teach you different techniques to use to release stress and recharge your batteries.

TAKE A DEEP BREATH

Breathe! It's so simple, yet many of us fail to do it properly. Breathing will naturally become shallow when you're under stress, but if you get into a habit of breathing like this you can end up feeling worked up when there's no need. When exercising, relaxing or in everyday activities, you should learn the habit of breathing so deeply that your abdomen rises as well as your chest.

WINDING DOWN

If you have trouble sleeping, develop a bedtime ritual. Don't charge around until the last minute, then expect to drop off easily. Wind down for half an hour with a warm bath or shower and enjoy a few minutes bedtime reading or talking. Don't watch television in bed as you'll give your brain the wrong signals. A warm, milky drink helps (but don't have too much sugar).

www.crownsportsplc.com

Dragons
HEALTH CLUBS

Bedford
81-83 Kimbolton Road
Bedford MK41 9DL
(01234) 354363

Dragons Brentwood
Chindits Lane
Warley, Brentwood
Essex CM14 5LF
(01277) 202088

Burnham
Buckingham Avenue
Trading Estate
Slough SL1 4JB
(01753) 553888

Derby
Carrington Street
Castle Ward
Derby DE1 2ND
(01332) 381451

Epsom
27 Ruxley Lane
Ewell, Surrey KT19 0JB
(020) 8393 6011

Gatwick
Copthorne Road
Copthorne, Crawley
West Sussex RH10 3PG
(01342) 715022

Guildford
Epsom Road, Merrow
Guildford, Surrey GU4 7AA
(01483) 458811

Hove
St Heliers Avenue, Hove
East Sussex BN3 5RE
(01273) 724211

Leamington Spa
46-48 Bedford Street
Leamington Spa
Warwickshire
CV32 5DT
(01926) 883679

Leeds
Haworth Lane, Yeadon
Leeds LS19 7EN
(0113) 239 1155

Lincoln
Witham Park House
Witham Park, Waterside
South Lincoln LN5 7JP
(01522) 568755

Maidstone
Mill Meadow, St Peter Street
Maidstone, Kent ME16 0SX
(01622) 681987

Muswell Hill
Hillfield Park, Muswell Hill
London N10 3PJ
(020) 8444 8212

Northwood
Chestnut Avenue, Northwood
Middlesex HA6 1HR
(01923) 840214

Orpington
Sandy Lane, St Pauls Cray
Orpington, Kent BR5 3HY
(01689) 874884

Purley
33 Imperial Way, Purley Way
Croydon, Surrey CR0 4RR
(020) 8686 8811

Rugby
Webb Ellis Road, Rugby
Warwickshire CV22 7AU
(01788) 540523

Western Avenue
Rowdell Road, Northolt
Middlesex UB5 6AG
(020) 8841 5611

Milton Keynes
Brickhill Street, Willen Lake
Milton Keynes MK15 0DS
(01908) 295699

Chester
Wrexham Road,Chester
Cheshire CH4 7QP
(01244) 683999

Southport
Fairways, North Promenade
Southport, Merseyside PR8 1RY
(01704) 532999

Sale
Whitehall Road, Brooklands
Sale, Cheshire M33 3NL
(0161) 972 8999

fitnessexpress

Ardsley House Hotel
Doncaster Road, Barnsley
South Yorkshire S71 5EH
(01226) 329010

Barnham Broom Hotel
Honingham Road, Barnham
Broom, Norwich NR9 4DD
(01603) 759741

Barnsdale Hall Hotel
Exton, Nr Oakham
Rutland LE15 8AB
(01572) 771314

Bentley Hotel
Newark Road, South Hykeham
Lincoln LN6 9NH
(01522) 823200

Broadland Holiday Village
Marsh Road, Oulton Broad
Lowestoft NR33 9JY
(01502) 517452

Forest Pines
Ermine Street, Broughton
Nr Brigg, Lincolnshire
DN20 0AQ
(01652) 651538

Manchester Airport Marriott
Hale Road, Hale Barns,
Altrincham, Cheshire
WA15 8XW
(0161) 904 5050

Kelling Heath Health Club
Weybourne, Sheringham
Norfolk NR25 7HW
(01263) 589919

Knights Hill Hotel
South Wootton, Kings Lynn
Norfolk PE30 3HQ
(01553) 670991

Swallow Hotel Nelson
Prince of Wales Road,
Norwich, Norfolk
NR1 1DX
(01603) 214440

Park Farm Hotel
Hethersett, Norwich
Norfolk NR9 3DL
(01603) 812775

Stoke By Nayland Golf Club
Keepers Lane, Leavenheath
Colchester C06 4PZ
(01206) 265820

Ufford Park Hotel
Yarmouth Road
Ufford, Woodbridge
Suffolk IP12 1QW
(01394) 386449

LE CLUB
HEALTH & FITNESS

Copthorne Hotel Birmingham
Paradise Circus
Birmingham B3 3HJ
(0121) 200 2727

Copthorne Hotel Cardiff Caerdydd
Copthorne Way, Culverhouse Cross
Cardiff CF5 6DH
(0292) 0294 3160

Copthorne Hotel Effingham Park
Gatwick, Copthorne
West Sussex RH10 3EU
(01342) 712138

Copthorne Hotel Manchester
Clippers Quay, Salford Quays
Manchester M5 2XP
(0161) 873 7321

Copthorne Hotel Merry Hill Dudley
The Waterfront, Level Street
Brierley Hill, Dudley DY5 1UR
(01384) 844601

Copthorne Hotel Newcastle
The Close, Quayside
Newcastle Upon Tyne NE1 3RT
(0191) 222 0333

Copthorne Hotel Plymouth
Armada Way
Plymouth PL1 1AR
(01752) 631250

Copthorne Hotel Slough Windsor
Cippenham Lane, Slough
Windsor SL1 2YE
(01753) 607344

Millenium Madejski Hotel
Madejski Stadium
Reading RG2 0FL
(0118) 925 3844

INDEX

A
abdominal exercises 70-71
   strength 39, 49,
aerobic
   equipment 72-81
   exercise 72-81, 89
affirmation 14
alcohol 23, 87
arm exercises
   shoulder strength 46-47
   lat pull down 66-67
aromatherapy 92

B
back, care of 11, 24-25, 44
back exercises
   seated row 60-61
   strengthening 42-44
   stretching 30, 32, 33, 34, 51
benefits of exercise 7, 11, 53
blood pressure 11, 24, 46
breathing 21, 23, 46, 56, 74, 93
buttocks exercises
   strengthening 48

C
calories 76, 83-85
carbohydrates 84
cardiovascular exercise 11, 72-81
chest exercises
   chest press 58-59
   press-ups 40-41
cholesterol 11
circulation 27
clothes 20, 28, 56, 76
confidence 7-8, 12, 18, 38, 52-53
cross trainer 80-81

cycling 12, 23, 27, 28, 72-73, 78-79, 80, 88

D
diabetes 11, 24
diet 7, 72, 82-87
drinks 21, 23, 87

E
eating habits 7, 14, 23, 82-87
elliptical trainer 81
energy 7-8, 11, 12, 84, 85
essential oils 92
exercise
   aerobic/cardiovascular 72-81
   ball 57
   benefits 7, 11, 24-25, 53
   class 12, 23
   equipment 13, 54-81
   home 12, 38-51
   myths 13
   programme 12, 20-21, 23, 25, 52-53
   safety 24-25, 26-27, 28, 36-37
exertion, levels of 36-37, 72

F
fat 11, 43, 54, 83, 85
fitness improvement 26-37
flexibility 11, 28-35
footwear 75, 76

G
goal setting 14
goals 12, 16-17, 18

H
hamstrings 74, 78, 80
   strengthening 48
health clubs 13, 23, 35, 38-39, 54-71, 74, 76, 88, 90-91, 92, 94
health check 24-25
heart disease 24, 82
heart rate 21, 37, 72
home exercise 38-51

I
injury 28
indoor bike 79
instructor, fitness 13, 38, 56, 64, 74-75

J
jogging 28, 76-77
joints
   impact 78, 80-81
   locking 41

L
leg exercises
   cross trainers 80-81
   cycling 78-79
   inner thigh 68
   outer thigh 69
   leg curl 62-63
   leg press 64-65
   running 76-77
   walking 74-75
ligaments 11

M
massage 92-93
minerals 86
muscles 11, 21, 26-27, 28-35, 38-51, 54-71, 76, 90-91

INDEX

abdominal70-71
fatigue 64
stiffness 58, 78

N
neck stretch 50
negative thoughts 18-19
nutrition 82-87

O
osteoporosis 11,

P
Pilates 8, 35
planning 14-15, 86-87
positive thinking 11, 14, 18-19
posture 44, 54, 60,74
power-walking 74
press-ups 40-41
protein 85

Q
quadriceps 74, 78, 80

R
relaxation 35, 88-93
repetitions 56
resistance equipment 22, 54-71

rest 88-93
reward 22
    points 22-23
running 12, 72, 76-77, 80

S
safety 24-25, 26-27
sauna 90-91
sets 56
shoulder exercises
    shoulder strength 33, 34, 46-47
    high pulls 60-61
sleep 54, 88, 93
smoking 23
spa bath 90-91
steamroom 23, 90-91
stress 11, 88
stretching 11, 23, 26-27, 28-35, 88
    back 30, 32, 33, 34, 51
    neck 50
    shoulders 33, 34
    sides and groin 29
    thighs 31
strength
    exercises 38-49, 54-71
sweating 21, 76

swimming 22, 23, 80, 89

T
thigh exercises 31, 45
time to exercise 17, 20
training log 17, 22, 38
treadmill 76

V
visualisation 14, 18
vitamins 85, 86
vitamin supplements 86

W
walking 11, 12, 27, 36, 72, 73, 74-75, 80
warm-up and cool-down 26-27, 78-79
water, drinking 21, 23, 87
weight loss 52-53, 82-83

Y
yoga 35, 54

REFERENCES

Be Your Best, Sally Gunnell with Kathryn Leigh (Thorsons)
Nutrition cards (The Lawn Tennis Association, London)
Personal Trainer Manual (American Council on Exercise)
Modern Principles of Athletic Training, Klafs and Arnheim (US Edition)
Textbook of Work Physiology, Astrand, Rodahl 1986 (McGraw Hill)
The Merck Manual of Medical Information, Merck (Simon and Schuster)
All photographs by Clive Corless